Look What the Lord Has Done

by

David B. Ward

author**HOUSE™**

1663 LIBERTY DRIVE, SUITE 200
BLOOMINGTON, INDIANA 47403
(800) 839-8640
WWW.AUTHORHOUSE.COM

First published by AuthorHouse 02/22/05

ISBN: 1-4208-3422-3 (sc)

Library of Congress Control Number: 2005901670

Printed in the United States of America
Bloomington, Indiana

This book is printed on acid-free paper.

Dedication

This chronicle of miraculous moments in our lives is dedicated to the glory of God. Over the years we have been the beneficiaries of the largesse of divine grace, infinite mercy and boundless love that only God can provide. These accounts are but a portion of the many blessings we have had showered upon us. Some cannot be told in this life, others are yet to come. We feel that we are God's favorite children. If such bounty was not available to all we might feel guilty for having so much. We can only keep the open secret that God's grace is sufficient to all our needs, and remain in wonder at Him. The following creed abides with us and will be our shelter in any storms we may face:

*There is only one God, and
His name is Jesus!
Jesus is the best friend
you could ever have.*

There is nothing too hard for God.

David & Bonnie Ward

Foreword

John concluded his Gospel by writing, "And there are also many other things which Jesus did, the which, if they should be written every one, I suppose that even the world itself could not contain the books that should be written..." You hold in your hands one of the books that chronicles the miracle working power of our Lord and Savior - like John, in part, rather than the whole. Look What The Lord Has Done starts with the early family years of David and Bonnie Ward. It journeys through their many years of foreign missions service. It is a testimony - personal and powerful - of the many miracles God has wrought - from healings to deliverances, protection and provision. These are their stories - These are His-story! To God be the glory - great things He hath done!

T. F. Tenney

Table of Contents

As Al and Martha watched Mary Ann approach her first birthday, the prospects of their child learning to walk were dim indeed...Hope rose and fell, but God did not waver. He never does.

Baby Steps

The fourth addition to the family of Al and Martha Banta was a pretty little girl named Mary Ann. She arrived in the seventh year of their marriage, making two girls and two boys in their happy home. The Bantas lived in Columbus, Georgia at the time, since Al was in the Air Force and stationed nearby.

Now this was a happy addition because the Bantas wanted children; the more the merrier. Martha loved children, and her desire for a big family came from early beginnings.

Once, while she was working as a nurse in Pasadena, California, Martha went to Sister Willie Johnson, an Evangelist well known to Martha's family. Sister Willie had often preached for Martha's father, Pastor Harper Rose, in the little village of Jewett, Ohio. Martha was single at the time, but her vision of a house full of happy children was already fully formed. Getting a chance to speak with Sister Willie, Martha earnestly shared her request; "Sister Willie, please pray that I will have children." Sister Willie responded just as earnestly, "Honey, I will pray for you to get a husband!"

Soon after, Martha's friend at her job introduced her to her brother, Al. Al wasn't in the church, but he went because he wanted to be with Martha. Soon Al was born again and within a year they were married. Years later when Martha met Sister Willie she showed her a picture of her five children. "Whoops, I prayed too big a prayer for you!" Sister Willie exclaimed. Martha couldn't have been happier.

Martha's sister, Ella May Stark, worked for an Osteopath in Wheeling, West Virginia. One day Martha was discussing with the Doctor about her first born, David. David was very small at the time and had a serious hernia. Doctor Graham was lecturing her about the seriousness of David's condition. He insisted that the child needed an operation. Martha, who was a registered nurse, understood the situation well. She and Al had decided to trust God, however, and that was that. In his frustration Dr. Graham asked Martha, "And what would you do if your child was born with a clubbed foot?" "I would trust God to heal it", was Martha's reply. David was healed, and Mary Ann was born with a clubbed foot.

Morning after morning Martha went to the crib of her little baby, expecting to find her miracle. Time and again she found Mary Ann still in possession of the deformity she was born with. Finally, when the child was about six months old, they went to a Doctor to get his advice. "Nothing can be done", he told them, "but she will be alright; she has beautiful eyes". So, by choice or necessity, faith was their course.

As Al and Martha watched Mary Ann approach her first birthday, the prospects of their child learning to walk were dim indeed. Each morning when Martha went to take her baby from the crib, her eyes habitually went to the child's feet. One was fashioned so perfectly while the other taunted her confidence in God with it's misshapen form. Daily Martha laid her hand on the feet of her baby and prayed for a miracle. Hope rose and fell, but God did not waver. He never does.

How thrilling it was to the heart of this dear Mother when one morning, eyes still heavy with sleep, she went to attend to her baby. With the habit born of many such mornings, Martha looked her child over. When her eyes reached the pink bare feet of her baby, she beheld two perfect little feet. Before long Mary Ann was adding to the patter of feet in the Banta house; eight perfect little feet, with more to come.

A few years passed and Mary Ann was going to school. In the third grade, she was as full of life and energy as any. In the spring the children were able to play outdoors during recess, and they were boisterous and busy, venting the pent up energy of a long winter. On the playground the children were busy in their various games. One boy, swinging a baseball bat, lost his grip and the bat went sailing across the school yard. Mary Ann unknowingly moved into the path of the missile and it thumped soundly against her skull. She dropped like a broken doll onto the playground and lay still.

Attempts to reach Martha were unsuccessful. She had gone out and no one knew where she was. Coming out with the rest of the fifth grade class for recess, Mary Ann's sister Bonnie May was informed that her sister had been hurt and had been taken to the teacher's lounge. Bonnie May found her lying on a ledge under the window where she had been placed after being scooped up and carried by one of the high school students.

Finally they carried her out to a car to find a doctor. Mary Ann was unconscious, being held by the high school boy in the back seat of the car. Bonnie went with her as they drove to the Doctor's office in Jewett. He wasn't there. Down the winding road they continued to Scio, the next town about six miles away. Again the doctor wasn't in, but they were informed that he had gone to the Pottery and could be found there. They bumped over multiple railroad tracks and down a dirt road. Mary Ann was not restrained, not on a board or with a collar to protect her from further injury. Finally they carried her once more to where the doctor could be found. He told them to take her straight to the hospital. There they found to his horror that her skull was fractured half way around her head.

At last they managed to reach her father. "Which daughter is it?" he asked. The doctor answered, "I'm not sure, she's the one with freckles". Somehow a message reached Pastor Rose, Mary Ann's grandfather. He came with Al and Martha to the hospital. Brother Clinton Smith, an elder in the church, joined them and they prayed. They prayed the effectual fervent prayer of faith. Two days later she was ready to go home. No fracture. No swelling of the brain; just an active little girl who wanted to go home. They had to keep her an extra day because another child had come in with a highly contagious disease and they needed to make sure Mary Ann didn't catch it. She didn't.

The item of this day was about the huge wave hurtling westward across the Pacific Ocean, and the troop ship that was in its path. "Martha is on that ship, and I must pray."

Coming Home

Martha Rose graduated from nursing school in Wheeling, West Virginia in 1943. Before long she was enlisted in the United States Army, serving as a nurse to the wounded heroes of the Second World War. This took her to many places, notably the Far East. Traveling to Japan and the Philippines, she saw much of the devastation and death that was the result of vicious conflict. Certainly this made her the object of many prayers, including those of her parents, Harper and Lottie Rose.

Harper Rose pastored a church in the little village of Jewett, Ohio, but he was a man of God with a vision for the world. His little church that normally ran to forty or so on a Sunday morning was one of the strongest supporters of Foreign Missions in the Ohio District. He was also a man of prayer who commonly spent long hours of the night in prayer and study, sleeping in cat naps during the day. He saw many prayers answered but you seldom heard about it from him. His passion in life was to bring men to the born-again experience of salvation. And at this point in time, his dear Martha was not yet saved.

It caused no small stir when the letter came announcing Martha's return from her tour in the vast Pacific theater. She named the troop ship she would be on and gave the date of her arrival on the west coast. This was delightful news to Harper and Lottie; their Martha was coming home.

Somewhere in the process, the Army took over. As happens so many times, plans were changed. Oh Martha was still returning to the States, but on a different troop ship. With no time to get this change of plans communicated to her loved ones, Martha got on the ship with hundreds of others like her. Days of travel with little to do and not much space to do it in seemed to make a long journey longer. But Martha was going home, and that was what counted.

In the course of the journey something happened that changed everything. Somewhere in the great northwest, in the area of Alaska and the Aleutian Islands, the earth gave a mighty heave. Rocks trembled and land masses groaned far away from the boredom of the troop ship in the Pacific. A mighty wall of water began to sweep across the ocean at a speed much faster than any ship, destroying everything in its path. That wave went all the way to Hawaii and beyond. And Martha's ship was directly in its path.

Back home in Jewett, Harper and Lottie Rose lived their lives as many did in the times. News came first on the radio and just about everybody listened to the newscaster to know what was going on in the world. The item of this day was about the huge wave hurtling westward across the Pacific Ocean, and the troop ship that was in its path. The newscaster named the ship, and Harper Rose became gravely concerned. "Martha is on that ship", he told his wife Lottie. "Martha is on that ship and is in real danger". "No, Harper, here is her letter. It says she is going to be on another ship. Surely Martha is O.K.", replied Lottie. Harper was adamant. "Martha is on that ship, and I must pray". With that he left the room and went to talk to his God.

On the ship the passengers were told of the situation. The wave was coming, that was sure. It would sink the boat, and there was no way to escape. They were ordered to their bunks to wait; to wait for a certain death. There was nothing else to do. No doubt many met at the throne of God that day. If they could have been aware, they would have seen Harper Rose somewhere close to the throne, pleading for Martha and her shipmates.

It is amazing to consider the power of prayer. The effectual fervent prayer of a righteous man avails much. (James 5:16) Another scripture gives a specific promise of answered prayer.

I Jn 5:14-16
14 *And this is the confidence that we have in him, that, if we ask any thing according to his will, he heareth us:*

15 *And if we know that he hear us, whatsoever we ask, we know that we have the petitions that we desired of him.*

16 *If any man see his brother sin a sin which is not unto death,* **he shall ask, and he shall give him life for them that sin not unto death.** *There is*

*a sin unto death: I do not say that he shall pray
for it.(KJV)*

Harper Rose never told whether he called on this promise in his plea for the ship. Perhaps in his wonderful relationship with God he held a special advantage. But it was life he got that day, life for Martha and hundreds of others.

Trapped in a steel box lumbering clumsily across the waves, the troops waited for a fury more powerful than the atomic bomb to be unleashed upon them. Thoughts of home and loved ones gave little comfort against the gloom that crept silently through the ship. Life jackets were donned in a futile protest against the death that was surely coming to them. And then the wave came.

Came and went is what it did, all the way to the Hawaiian Islands, wreaking havoc and damage like another Pearl Harbor. However, when the wave came to the ship Martha was on, it did an incredible thing. The force of the wave plunged down into the depths of the ocean as it approached the troop ship. The ship was not swamped with the tons of water they expected. It did not pitch with sickening violence and break up as they supposed it would. The ship sailed on and somewhere on the other side of the ship's course the wave re-surfaced and raced on its way to the west.

Martha and hundreds like her were saved from certain death and few could explain how it happened. Martha was coming home.

Earnestly the seeker prayed and worshipped. Quickly she felt the wonderful presence of God. She thought she was done.

You Wanted It; You Got It

Granny Ward excelled in cooking and hospitality, and she had a passion for witnessing. It didn't matter if you were a stranger. Strangers were just friends you didn't know yet, and they needed to know about Jesus. Often the pastor would call on Granny Ward to lead testimony service. Sometimes the anointing would take over and she would preach, though she would never have assumed to call it that. Bro. Kinzie would just sit back and urge her on.

One Sunday morning there was a visitor in the service. Granny saw her and found her way over to greet her. "Oh you should come back tonight," she enthused, "Our night services are so good, lots of good music and you will really enjoy it." The visitor replied that she would indeed like to return that night, but that she could not drive at night due to a night blindness problem. Granny would not be denied; "You just come ahead, it will be daylight when you get here. Then after service you can come home with me." She came.

We were visiting at my parents' home that weekend and took note that the visitor was there; nothing unusual about that. We didn't think much about it. The next morning we went on our way, and left Granny to her guest.

The first thing she did was fix breakfast. There was one thing you did at Granny Wards' house; you ate. And you certainly ate breakfast, there was no way out. So the visitor sat down to eggs and sausage with biscuits and gravy and maybe some sliced tomatoes. If you haven't had milk gravy on fresh tomatoes you just don't know what you are missing.

After clearing up the dishes the two of them sat down together and opened the Bible. Granny directed her to the book of Acts. She read of how the Apostles laid hands on people and they received the baptism of the Holy Ghost, speaking with tongues. As granny read her visitor interrupted her; "That's it. That is what I want. I want the Holy Ghost."

Now Granny was all for that, no doubt. However the swiftness of her visitors' response took her back a bit. "Well, I guess what we need to do is call the pastor and let him come and pray with you", Granny offered. This lady would have nothing of that, however. "No, that is not necessary. You can just lay hands on me like the Apostles did, and I will receive the Holy Ghost. Go on, you can do it", she insisted.

Well this was a new one on Granny. She had been around the church for a while and had seen and done a lot of things, but this laying on of hands was a new one for her. There was no way out. This lady was not going to be denied so they may as well just get on with it.

"Just kneel down here at the couch and lift up your hands. Now begin to praise the Lord and He will give you the Holy Ghost", Granny instructed. No doubt she breathed a silent prayer for divine help as the lady began to pray: "Lord, I have opened my mouth and now I really need you to do this".

Earnestly the seeker prayed and worshipped. Quickly she felt the wonderful presence of God. She thought she was done. Starting to get up, she felt the touch of hands made strong by long years of working on the farm and at the hospital. "No, you're not done, honey. Just keep on praising God", Granny insisted. Back on her knees the visitor started again. Again the wonderful presence of God washed over her. Again she started to rise and felt herself urged back to her knees to continue her praying. "You want the Holy Ghost, well you may as well just keep on until you get it", Granny insisted. The one thing Granny understood about seeking God was that you didn't give up until you got what you were after. She had received the Holy Ghost the first time she prayed for it, so she had pure faith that everyone should have it. So up and down went the visitor until she broke out speaking in another tongue. Then and only then did Granny allow her to get up. Much rejoicing ensued and then Granny allowed her to be on her way.

How well I remember the timing of this event. It was only the night before that for the first time ever a man climbed out of a space ship and walked on the moon. His experience there, however, had nothing on Granny. Man had launched a man and landed him on the moon. Granny had helped to launch a soul into the kingdom of God.

*Contacting an evangelist, we held prayer meetings
and did our best to enthuse the saints of our little
congregation to expect a miracle. We didn't dream
we were about to get four of them.*

Our First Revival

In August, 1969 we packed up everything we owned in an eight foot U-Haul trailer and moved from Ohio to Torrington, Connecticut. I was soon to be the new pastor of the church in Torrington; all this at the tender age of twenty-two. Bonnie wasn't even that old. We had been married almost a year and there was a passion for God in our hearts. We wanted to do something for God and this seemed like the time and place to do it. Friends and family who loved us did their best to talk us out of taking such a bold step at our age and inexperience. We knew we had heard from God and told them, "Thank you very much but this has got to be done".

Our confidence was bolstered with the promise of a job working for the Torrington Bearing Company. There was a little congregation meeting in Litchfield Chapel in East Litchfield, on the edge of Torrington. The building was a historical site and we got to use it for just maintenance and utilities. So with joy and wonder we rushed in. The angels, much wiser than we, had no choice but to follow us.

Our time in Torrington was a wonderful experience and quite an education for us. It was the first of many such adventures. God was good to us and things were going pretty well. Finally the time came when we felt we were ready to have a revival.

Contacting an evangelist, we held prayer meetings and did our best to enthuse the saints of our little congregation to expect a miracle. We didn't dream we were about to get four of them.

Pop Davis

Elmore Davis was a genuine Connecticut Yankee. Fiercely independent and of a singular bent of mind, Pop Davis knew what he believed and didn't mind saying so. Pop was a recent convert to Pentecost. He believed in one God, was baptized, paid his tithes faithfully and came to church regularly. He had not received the Holy Ghost yet and so was a prime target for our revival. On Saturday before the revival services started we invited Brother & Sister Davis to our house for lunch. We often visited their home and wanted to make sure that they were ready for the revival experience. We had a nice visit. As they were leaving our house, I spoke up and said, "Brother Davis, I hope you receive the Holy Ghost in this revival". Pop fired back at me in his usual "shoot from the hip" fashion; "I don't know if there is such a thing as the baptism of the Holy Ghost". I assured him that we would be praying for him, and I wasn't kidding.

The next morning we welcomed the saints to Sunday School and it was apparent that something was afoot. Brother & Sister Davis came in and sat down in their usual places, but he didn't look right at all. His face was read and swollen, his eyes almost shut. He was in obvious extreme discomfort. At prayer time Bro. Davis came forward for healing. This was something he believed in. We prayed our best healing prayer and Pop didn't get an ounce of relief. After service they went straight home and we looked forward to the beginning of the revival that night.

When service time arrived that evening the saints all gathered, including Elmore & Francis Davis. He looked pretty much the same, all red-faced and miserable. The evangelist ministered and gave an altar call at the close of his message, inviting people to come and receive the Holy Ghost. To my shock Pop Davis was the first one in the altar. Immediately I went to him and began to pray with him. Within about five minutes Pop Davis was speaking with other tongues. When he received the Holy Ghost, the redness and swelling left his face. It was like watching a thermometer go down quickly. When things calmed down a bit I couldn't help but ask him, "Pop, what happened? Yesterday you didn't believe in the Holy Ghost and today you have it!" His reply was a testimony to answered prayer. In my youthful zeal I had prayed for Pop earnestly, "God, give him the Holy Ghost whatever it takes".

What it took was for Pop to get utterly miserable. He explained that, after they had left our house the previous day, he did some work on his car. Pop was allergic to motor oil. After working on his car he began to swell up and turn red. That night he had not been able to sleep. Failing to get the hoped-for healing on Sunday morning, Pop went home in misery. Finally on Sunday afternoon Pop prayed, "God, if you will let me get some sleep, I will seek for the Holy Ghost". He then immediately went to sleep. That night he not only received the Holy Ghost, but got his healing. He didn't need to be miserable any more.

Sister White

Vina White lived in a run down clap-board house in the worst area of the city. We picked her up for every service. She was seventy-five years old and couldn't hear very well. Sometimes she would disturb the service with her stage whisper voice, "Huh, what chapter did he say—where is that book?" I honestly thought that she came to church just to get out of the squalor she lived in for just a little while.

As our revival progressed, it became obvious that she was touched by God. One of the sisters in the church went to her during altar service one night and asked her if she would like to receive the Holy Ghost. She replied that she had never been baptized. Sister White had a great fear of going under water left over from a bad experience when she was a child. "Oh, you can receive the Holy Ghost even before you are baptized", she was told. Now you have to understand something about Sister White. She had the purest faith of anyone I have ever seen. When Sister White came for healing, she got healed. When she prayed about an issue, it got dealt with. When she was told that she could receive the Holy Ghost even before being baptized, she immediately lifted hands and began to speak with tongues! Strengthened by this new power, she was soon baptized. Years later when we came to Torrington for a Missionary service, we went and found Sister White in the nursing home. She was over ninety years old by then but recognized us immediately. She was a happy lady, with all the faith and light in her eyes that we had known. She was on her way to a better place, and she just knew it.

Sister Dubourg

Sister Dubourg was originally from Alabama and you knew it when she spoke. This alone made her unique in the setting of New England. She was seventy-five and a half, she would let you know, and she took delight in holding it over Sister Whites' head that she was her elder. This lady lived with her daughter, who took her entire Social Security check for her upkeep. Once in a while she would do some ironing or such for her daughter and would get a little money for it.

Once in the middle of the week I realized that I needed to get some gas for our car, but I didn't have any money. It was doubtful that the car could keep going until pay day, and it was Wednesday night. Deciding to trust God and use the gas to go to church, I figured I could walk to work if I had to. Sister Dubourg met me at the door with excitement. "Brother Ward, Brother Ward, I have got something for you. Today I did some ironing for my daughter. She paid me four dollars, and I am going to split with you!"

Each night of the revival Sister Dubourg would pray earnestly. "Lord I believe", she would repeat endlessly in her best Alabama drawl. I personally wished she would say something else, but obviously I was not in charge of Sister Dubourgs' prayers. After several nights of this unchanging exercise, I witnessed her moment of faith. Pausing for a moment, she got a look of surprise and excitement and blurted out, "Lord, I do believe!" The next words she spoke were in another tongue while she ran about as fast as her seventy-five and a half years old legs would take her. Sister Dubourg had finally come to her moment of faith.

Sister Davis

Francis Davis was as sweet as her husband Pop Davis was independent. She never spoke very loudly, and certainly never gave anyone the first minutes trouble. Francis would come to the altar and immediately be surrounded by a sweet presence of the Lord. Night after night, however, Francis went home without the Holy Ghost.

Toward the close of the revival services we were excited to have several visitors come to our meeting. When the altar call was given, every one of them came forward. From that point everything went sour. We couldn't seem to get a prayer past the ceiling. Nothing we tried seemed to have any effect. We went home frustrated and confused that night, but determined to do something about it. "I don't know what you are going to do," I told the evangelist, "but I am going to pray until we get the victory over this." Later we learned that the visitors were Satan worshippers who came to shut us down. In our inexperience we had not discerned it.

The next day we went to the church to pray. I felt impressed to pray for each family of the church in turn. As I prayed for them, I would petition God to tie the hands of the devil so that he could not work against them. With that prayer I would begin to pray in the spirit very forcefully, in a rebuking manner. This happened each time I prayed for another family. Feeling some victory, we went on our way and prepared for the service that evening.

That night Sister Davis came to the altar just like she always did. As usual, she soon was basking in the sweet presence of the Lord. But this night she began speaking with tongues. We were ecstatic with this victory. As I congratulated Sister Davis, she related the happenings of her day to me.

Sister Davis had been ironing in her front room. Looking up, she saw a hideous form before her. He was ugly and fearsome in appearance and manner, and she was afraid. Turning to call her husband, she looked back and the demon had disappeared. From this fearful experience she came to church and received the Holy Ghost. Pressed for details, Sister Davis told us that this happened about eleven in the morning. This was the very time we were praying at the church for God to tie the hands of the devil. I asked Sister Davis what he looked like, and she replied that he was hideous and fearful in appearance, but that she noticed his hands were crossed in front of him as if they were tied!

David B. Ward

Now when all of this happened I was about twenty four years old. The average age of those who received the Holy Ghost in the revival was seventy! We went on to see many more receive the Holy Ghost in many different situations, but we have never seen another revival quite like our first one.

By the end of the Sunday School session I was totally confused. It was obvious that God was working. Why didn't we have anyone receive the Holy Ghost?

The Number Six

Orla MacDonald was a solid saint. She and her husband Larry anchored the Sunday School staff, raised a family of good kids, labored in fund raising and witnessing; they were just the kind of people a pastor hoped to find. Larry MacDonald was raised in Pentecost and was sensitive in the spirit. He could be counted on to give sage advice and follow the Holy Ghost.

One day I went to the post office and found a letter in the box addressed to "The True Church". Out of all the churches in Torrington they put the letter in our box. The letter was from a member of a United Pentecostal Church in Maine. They did not know if that kind of church existed in Torrington, Connecticut. They just prayed and asked God to send the letter to the right place. In the letter they explained that they had grandchildren in Torrington. The kids were in a hopeless spiritual environment, with no likelihood of going to any church. We were asked to find these kids and please take them to our church.

I passed the letter on to Brother Larry, who informed me that he had already found the children in his outreach labors. The children were coming to church on a regular basis. This was exciting to a church of thirty to thirty-five people, and especially so to Bro. Larry and Sister Orla.

One Saturday afternoon Sister Orla called me. She told me that she had been praying and that God had spoken to her. She sounded very excited. Of course I asked her what the Lord had spoken to her and when she told me I was defeated as to how to respond. "The Lord gave me the number six", she said. I thought, Oh no, this solid saint has gone wacky. "What do you think that means Sister MacDonald?" I asked her. "I believe we are going to have six people receive the Holy Ghost in the church tomorrow", she replied with excitement. Now we had never had that many people receive the Holy Ghost in a whole revival, let alone in just one day. Carefully I tried to put this in perspective. "Well Sister MacDonald, God is certainly able. You just keep on praying." Not for a minute did I believe we were going to have six get the Holy Ghost in one day. I just hoped that I could prepare Sister Orla for the let down she was sure to experience when it didn't happen. I thought perhaps I should have a talk with Brother Larry to see if he could stabilize her a little bit.

The next morning we went to church as usual. We normally had everybody, including the children, for a time of worship and then dismissed the children to their classes. This morning was no different. However, as the service progressed, the presence of God became so powerful that I began to believe Sister Orla's word of faith. Anxious to follow the leading of the spirit, I dismissed the children to their classes. For about an hour we worshipped and prayed in the adult class. There were several there who needed to be filled with the spirit. Now this is something God has blessed me to do, so I began to work with them, doing everything I knew how to do that they might be filled. The presence of God was mighty. The people prayed earnestly. I did everything I knew how to do. Not one of them received the Holy Ghost.

By the end of the Sunday School session I was totally confused. It was obvious that God was working. Why didn't we have anyone receive the Holy Ghost? By now the children were coming back into the sanctuary. I was trying to put the best face I could on what had happened, but frankly I was clueless as to what was happening. Hurrying to a dismissal prayer, I saw Brother Larry's hand go up. "Could I say something Brother Ward"? he asked. I was just glad to put the attention anywhere but on me so I was happy to let him speak. "I thought you would like to know," he explained, "this morning in the Junior Class we taught the lesson about people receiving the Holy Ghost. When we came to the part about the Apostles laying hands on the people to receive the Holy Ghost, we asked the children if any of them would like to receive it. Several of them raised their hands. We prayed for them, and six of them received the Holy Ghost."

Some of those kids who received the Holy Ghost that day were the ones the letter told us about. A prayer from Maine prompted a letter with no proper address to dispatch a saint to find kids we did not know. A word

David B. Ward

from the Lord to another saint alerted the pastor to the coming outpouring and he could not take it in. While we watched and wondered God made things happen in His own mysterious way.

Only Gods protecting hand can account for the change in our habits that night. Whatever caused the thieves to run away was on our side. To God be the thanks and the Glory!

Protected

Life in a place like Freetown, Sierra Leone can be pretty predictable. Located on the tip of western Africa, it is going to be hot. Sometimes it would be wet, especially between May and November, when you could count on it raining every day. During the time of the harmattan winds it would be dusty as the clouds rained down the dust it had picked up over the Sahara desert. Otherwise the ocean we could see from our house would keep rolling in. The sun would rise at six and go down at six. There were no malls to go to, no parks to enjoy and very little difference from one day to the next.

As Missionaries to Sierra Leone, we lived out of town close to the Bible School. Five days a week and two nights a week found us teaching prospective pastors. There were no other houses very close to ours, but we enjoyed the peace and quiet of country living while being fifteen minutes from the center of town.

Churches in many places in Africa have only one service on Sunday, but our practice in Sierra Leone was different. We had church every Sunday night as well as in the morning. We would move around the churches in the area, visiting a different church each Sunday.

Our habit was to stay a while after the service to be friendly with the saints. We didn't usually stay a very long time, but we made a point to stay a while and be friendly. Often on the way home from Sunday evening church we would stop at the post office. KLM Airlines came in on Sunday afternoon and sometimes we would have mail on Sunday night. Then there came a new ice cream shop with soft serve ice cream. This was a treat for us and we liked to stop for a cone. Reaching home on Sunday night we would usually go straight into the house. After having a cold drink, just before going to bed, I would put the car in the garage and lock the house. We were very predictable.

One night that all changed. I preached in Dworzak Farm church on the other side of Freetown. As soon as the altar service wound down I told Bonnie to get the baby ready so we could go home. "Aren't you going to stay and greet the saints?" she asked. "Nope, I want to go home", was all I replied. We got in the car and bumped down the road into town. "Are you O.K.?" Bonnie asked me. "I'm fine, just want to go home", I said again. "Want to check the post office?" came next. "Nope, I want to go home." A few moments passed and then, "How about getting an ice cream cone?" "Nope, I just want to go home", seemed to be all I wanted to say.

Arriving at the house I put the car in the garage and locked the house as I came in. Then we got a coke and sat down to relax. We had been home about ten minutes when we heard the watchman screaming, "Thief, thief." I looked through the windows of the house at the areas I could see outside. There was definitely something going on outside though I could not see very well. We turned the lights off in the house and left on the outside lights, making it difficult for anyone outside to see us. I told Bonnie to go into the kitchen pantry with the baby just in case bullets started flying. The girls were away in boarding school, so there was no worry there. Going to the back bedroom, I eased the curtains back and saw immediately in front of me a man with a pistol poised, ready to capture me if I came out of the back door. We prayed for protection and soon all became silent. I feared for the watchman but there was not one thing we could do for him.

About forty minutes passed and we heard a vehicle drive up in front of our house. A car horn sounded twice, car doors opened and closed and the car drove off. A little while later I opened a window a bit and called for the watchman. "Amadou!", I called. "Are you alright?" "Yes", he replied. "Where are the thieves?" I asked. "They done go", he replied in his native Krio tongue. Watchfully I opened the door and looked to Amadou. He had been cut when they wrestled away his machete, but otherwise was unhurt. He explained to me that the thieves, six of them, had come in over the front gate, not a difficult thing to do. However, later, they had fled the compound, going out over a high wall topped with broken glass. Since our house was built on the side of a hill, the back wall was about fifteen feet high. There was blood on the wall where they climbed in haste. The thieves had run as if afraid. Only heaven and the thieves know why.

If we had been our usual predictable selves that night, we would have arrived home at least a half hour later. The car would have been outside and the house would have been open. Only days before in the same area thieves had emptied houses and attacked the occupants.

Only Gods protecting hand can account for the change in our habits that night. Whatever caused the thieves to run away was on our side. To God be the thanks and the Glory!

God spoke back in simple terms; "You can stay home and take care of your children. Or, you can go to Africa and I will take care of them."

I Will Take Care of Them

In 1978, while pastoring in Ohio, we felt the call to Africa. This was quite a new direction for me. I never expected to be a foreign missionary. Before we were married, Bonnie asked me if I felt any direction towards being a missionary. "No, not me", I told her. I will go to the east coast and do home missionary work." And that is what we did, at first. Then we felt the call to foreign missions and for several months I sought the Lord about which part of the world we should go to. Finally the door opened to go to Africa, and I felt it was the right thing to do. "Bonnie, I believe God wants us to go to Africa", I confided one Sunday morning. "I know", she said. She then proceeded to tell me how that God had called her to Africa when she was a child. She was afraid to go alone and when I showed no inclination to do so she thought she was off the hook. However, now we were united in this calling, and things began to come together to get us there.

We were appointed to go to Sierra Leone, West Africa, at the General Conference in Salt Lake City,

31

Utah, 1979. Accordingly we resigned the pastorate of the church and got ourselves ready for deputation.

Somewhere along the line as we considered what we were doing the thought of our two little girls came into the picture. "Lord, I am willing to answer your call. If you need me to die in Africa, then so be it. But what about my little girls? They don't have a call to Africa. They are small and young. What about them?", so was my conversation with the Lord about the care of my children. God spoke back in simple terms; "You can stay home and take care of your children. Or, you can go to Africa and I will take care of them." Now that is not what I call a difficult choice. When something is the will of God, you do it. When God offers to take care of something for you, you let Him. So we went on our way rejoicing.

Arriving in Africa for the first time, we had no idea what to expect. When we met the Foreign Missions Board for appointment, one of the Board Members asked me if we had ever been anywhere outside the United States. Striving to be scrupulously honest before this august committee, I replied, "Well, we went to Niagara Falls on our honeymoon". They thought that was hilarious. Now, looking out of the window of the plane as it rolled along the tarmac, I was looking for lions and elephants, wondering if we would find a nice mud hut to live in. Clearly we were as green as grass. It wasn't just the children that God needed to take care of.

Moving into the call as well as the house and the work, we got along just fine. We were being carried all the way. I suppose we really thought it was this easy, as if we were doing it all. Our children made friends and seemed to be very happy with our new life.

After we had been in Africa close to two years, we decided that we needed to get physical examinations. There are a lot parasites, tropical diseases, etc. in West Africa and we just wanted to be sure we were doing OK. To get the examinations we had to go to Liberia, to the large ELWA Mission complex outside of Monrovia. The whole family went for testing, etc. and we were to go back after a day or so for the results. When I returned for the results, the receptionist told me that the doctor needed to speak with me. I was to go right in. Sitting down in his office, I was informed that our daughter Lori had some very disturbing symptoms. He had stayed up the entire night researching what he found in Lori. The diagnosis was chilling. "You need to take her to the US and find a Pediatric Endocrinologist", he advised. "Your daughter may have a tumor of the brain or pituitary gland", he told me. "She could become a giant or a dwarf, or even die". He instructed me to have her blood pressure checked. "If she has high blood pressure, I'm right". So I shared the news with Bonnie and Brother & Sister Hall. Sister Hall had a blood pressure cuff, and we played a game with the kids, checking their blood pressure. Lori was the only one with high blood pressure. It was on Bomi Mission we joined together with Missionaries Jim and Pat Hall in earnest prayer for Lori's miracle.

Soon Bonnie and the girls were on the way back to the States while I continued our work in Freetown. It seemed like an age passed before we knew any results of the testing done in America. All we knew was that the doctor said our little girl might be dying. All we trusted in was the promise of God to take care of our children.

Lori spent a couple of days in the hospital for the testing to be done. The days dragged on as I wondered what was happening. Communication was difficult in and out of Sierra Leone, and I didn't know if Bonnie had tried to reach me or not. Finally the report came in. "I don't know why you brought this little girl in; we can't find the problem you talked about. She is just fine."

Just one word: if you need something very precious to be well taken care of, give it to Jesus.

Note: About two years later we were on deputation in West Virginia. The pastor of the church in Huntington arranged for us to meet a Sunday School teacher in his church. This precious lady told us how, right at the time of our crisis with Lori, she had been wakened in the middle of the night. The name Sierra Leone came to her so forcefully that she could not sleep. Not knowing what it meant, she referred to an encyclopedia and learned that Sierra Leone is a country in West Africa. Inquiring into which missionaries were in Sierra Leone, she found that our family was there and that we had a six year old daughter, Lori. This sister was the teacher of the six year old class in their Sunday School. From that time she determined that their class would pray for Lori. Imagine looking for protection for your child's life and finding it in a group of six years olds!

The rain stopped. For as long as I preached that day,
it did not rain where we were gathered. Interestingly,
it did rain all around us. But we were protected!

Shelter in the Storm

By 1987 we were living in Kakamega, Kenya. We had been missionaries there for almost two years, and there was a great harvest. Week in and week out I went to the different areas of the region. Sometimes we had service in a mud church, sometimes in a market, or maybe under a tree.

Once I was preaching to about two hundred people who were seated under the shade of a spreading tree. To my back, just a few feet behind me stood a huge field of sugar cane. My message that day was about the one God. Everything seemed to be going just fine until suddenly the crowd separated into two sections, leaving a wide path between them. There was considerable excitement but it all happened so fast that I did not know the cause. Turning to one of the preachers beside me, I asked him what had happened. He told me that an eight foot black cobra had descended from the tree while I was preaching. The people saw it and gave the fellow a path into the cane field behind us. It happened so fast that many did not actually get a good look at the snake. They did not need much persuasion though and the reaction was instantaneous. When the people settled down I continued my message and all was well.

Some time later I was requested to preach in the city of Eldoret. It was a Sunday morning and as I drove to the city I saw that the sky promised rain. Arriving at the place for the service I learned that we would be meeting outdoors under a tree that gave partial shelter from the elements.

The service was opened and I was given a place of honor to sit under the shelter provided by the spreading branches of the tree. Now there was always a certain ceremony involved with meetings like this. It was a sectional rally, with saints and preachers from various locations around Eldoret in attendance. Sitting as comfortably as I could, I observed while this one was honored, that one gave his testimony etc.

Looking off into the distance I saw a dark specter of a huge storm cloud. It was quickly moving in our direction, and the prospects of finishing this service didn't look good. I decided that I would not be able to preach; it was going to rain.

The vain hope that the brethren might see the situation and move things along a bit more quickly appeared and quickly vanished in my mind. As the Kenyans had told me many times, there is no hurry in Africa.

Finally they announced that I would preach. Before I was able to finish greeting the people, I felt the first cold rain drops landing on the back of my neck as if they were guided missiles. Here it was. Thinking that these people deserved to believe that their missionary had enough sense to come in out of the rain, I opened my mouth to dismiss the service. "No, don't dismiss!" urged the voice of the spirit, "I want you to preach." I looked around and saw the dark spots growing in number as the rain increased. "Well, Lord", I replied under my breath, "I am ready to preach, but this rain is beyond my power." "I need you to stop the rain for as long as I preach, and then I will be glad to do it." The rain stopped. For as long as I preached that day, it did not rain where we were gathered. Interestingly, it did rain all around us. In a tight little circle around the 120 or so who were gathered there, it poured. In fact, it hailed, and the wind blew branches through the air space of our service, but not one drop fell in that circle. The wind was so strong that day that later we saw that trees had been blown over. But we were protected!

Finally I finished my message and prepared to give an altar call. To my horror it began to rain once more upon our service. Quickly I took hold of the presbyter, who was the closest preacher to me. "I made a mistake!" I confessed to him. "Pray with me for the rain to hold off until we get done praying!" In my haste I am not sure that I spoke to him in Swahili, and he understood little English. So we prayed together, me praying for the rain to hold off and my brother praying for who knows what; never mind, the rain stopped. Again the storm raged around us, hurling hail stones on a cold wind, and rain enough to soak us all, but we were untouched by the storm's fury.

We prayed for some time, and the Holy Ghost fell among us. After a while we counted thirty who had received the baptism of the Holy Ghost. That seemed to be the harvest, so I gave the signal for the people to stop praying. We did not use a loudspeaker that day, but we had arranged a signal. When it was time to stop praying we would beat the drum. This was the cue to bring the prayer to and end. Without the beating of the drum we never could have pierced the tumult of their earnest prayers. Then an amazing thing happened; the instant they began to beat the drum, as soon as we finished praying, the storm was unleashed upon us! We all scattered, racing to the nearest shelter from the lashing wind, soaking rain and hail stones the size of marbles. God had once more given us exactly what we asked.

Whatever storm may be on your horizon today, understand that there is an umbrella called grace that covers you. As long as you stand where the will of God has taken you, there is a host of angels urging you on; "Go ahead, God wants this to happen!" You are protected.

I spent many hours in the Intensive Care Unit, particularly for kidney dialysis. In the course of this treatment, my heart stopped beating. Bonnie was close by and saw the line go flat on the heart monitor.

Living Again

Deputation travel often has interesting twists and turns, and our furlough in 1989 was no exception. Brother J.P. Hughes, our Regional Director for Africa, requested us to change fields from Kenya to Tanzania. We loved Kenya and didn't really want to leave, but we dutifully consented to pray about it. Bonnie and I agreed together that, if the Foreign Missions Board requested us to go to Tanzania, we would consider it to be the will of God. We felt safe in that arrangement, because we never expected the board to make that request.

I was traveling by myself in the winter months. Sitting in the home of a long-time friend, Pastor Jim Fielders, I heard the phone ring. "It's for you", Brother Fielders told me. I took the phone and heard the voice of Missionary Director Harry Schism, "Brother Ward, I am sitting here with the entire Foreign Missions Board. The Board would like for you and Sister Ward to consider going to the country of Tanzania". I was stunned. "My goodness", I thought, "We are going to Tanzania". Well there wasn't much to think about. When you know the will of God, you just do it. Requesting a day to consult with Bonnie, I promised to let them know what we would do. However, the decision was already made by powers much higher than I, or the Foreign Missions Board for that matter.

We landed at Kilimanjaro International Airport on a Sunday afternoon. Bonnie, Lori, Andy and Rascal (our German Shepherd) were with me. We had the usual large amount of luggage that always accompanies a missionary going for an extended stay in a far away place. We were supposed to be met at the airport by a welcoming group including preachers, a choir, etc. However someone had misunderstood the time of arrival. Clearing immigration and customs, we searched in vain for a friendly face in the crowd. All we saw was everyone else leaving the airport.

As the population dwindled in the airport, it seemed wise to take things in our own hands. Negotiating as best we could in our Kenyan Swahili, we arranged for a pickup truck to carry us and our luggage to Moshi, about twenty-five miles away.

Bonnie and Lori sat in the cab of the pickup; Andy, Rascal and I climbed into the back with the luggage. So without the intended pomp and ceremony we arrived on the field anyway. God helped us to find where we needed to go, and so we began in Tanzania.

After about two years we returned from a trip to Musoma and Mwanza, on the shores of Lake Victoria. It was a long road trip on some pretty rough roads. We returned home exhausted from the rigors of the journey. Sometimes when we became so weary the residual presence of malaria in our bodies would cause a flare-up of the disease. Some time ensued and we traveled to Nairobi and back. Soon after arriving home I felt ill and suspected an episode of malaria was in progress. This was not an unusual occurrence, so we didn't think much about it. As I became more and more ill, we finally went to a clinic for a blood check. This confirmed that I had malaria, and the doctor gave me Phansadar, a sulfa based remedy for the malaria. After starting this treatment I became much sicker. I was sinking quickly into a dangerous state. Bonnie recognized in me some of the same symptoms she had seen in a dear friend of ours who died of malaria in Kenya. Finally, with little health care available in Tanzania, we decided to use our Medivac coverage and get me flown to Nairobi for treatment.

When the plane arrived at Wilson Airport, I was transferred to an ambulance and taken to Nairobi Hospital. There, I was admitted to the hospital and they began treatment immediately. When some tests came back the following day, we discovered that I not only had malaria, but was also suffering from hepatitis. This was no doubt the result of bad food or water. The timing was just right for me to have contracted hepatitis on our trip to western Tanzania. After some time Dr. Warshaw took Bonnie aside to explain the circumstances of my illness. He told her that, normally, the liver enzymes would measure at 100, and that if it reached 1,400 it would be fatal. Then he told her that mine were measuring at 9,000! Bonnie asked about getting me back to the US, and was told that I would not survive the trip. She was to inform the family and accept the inevitable. I was not going to make it. They transferred me to the High Dependency Unit. The doctor explained to Bonnie that my liver and kidneys were operating at about 15% of normal. I had turned quite yellow by this time, and my body had begun to swell. Eventually my tongue split from the swelling. Through all this I felt little pain or discomfort, primarily because I was in and out of consciousness. My treatment consisted of being dosed with many different medicines and being given kidney dialysis. The doctors were using every means they could to keep me alive, but the prognosis was bleak. I spent many hours in the Intensive Care Unit, particularly for kidney dialysis. In the course of this treatment, my heart stopped beating. Bonnie was close by and saw the line go flat on the heart monitor. When she brought this to the attention of the nurse, she was hustled out of the room. Another lady, who was also told to go out, told Bonnie that they were using the paddles on my chest. They got my heart going again and so continued treatment.

Our friends in Nairobi rallied to our cause. They provided a place for Bonnie to stay and accompanied her to and from the hospital many times. The missionaries and pastors offered prayer and visited the hospital, even though they were usually not allowed to see me for very long at a time. Prayer requests went back to the US and churches, Bible Schools and many friends went to prayer in my behalf.

For about three days and nights I was in a coma induced by the extreme levels of poison flooding through my system. The medical staff fought on in what they knew was a futile effort to save my life. During that time and afterward people of different racial and religious backgrounds offered prayer for my healing. Throughout this I was aware of little or nothing, and certainly remembered nothing. Our personal physician added to the advice of Dr. Warshaw. "He is terribly sick", she told Bonnie, and "You have to be prepared for what is going to happen". The doctors were very kind, but they were unanimous in their opinion that I was dying; it was just a matter of time.

During this ordeal Bonnie would get calls from the states inquiring about my condition. One night (Thursday) when I was in a coma, she went to bed wearily and went to sleep. At about 1 AM the phone rang. It was a pastor friend from Michigan who was wondering how I was doing. Bonnie spoke with him for a while and then after the call was wide awake. Deciding to spend the time in praying for me, she was brought up short by the voice of the Lord. "You are not permitted to ask for his life," spoke the spirit, "Whatever happens, you must worship me." Well, that is just what Bonnie did, entering a realm of worship that could only be described as the "high praises" of God. This is a costly but very rewarding endeavor.

On Saturday morning when she arrived at my bedside, Bonnie found me awake. My liver enzymes had gone from 9,000 to 200 in one night! The doctor explained to her that, while this certainly looked good, it could just be that my body was shutting down. He also told her that if I did survive, the high levels of toxins in my body had probably damaged my brain. We would just have to wait and see. Bonnie watched me for a while and saw that, not only did I seem to be in possession of my senses; I could even still speak Swahili!

Experiencing all this was something you don't forget. All that I can remember from the time I was comatose was the feeling of not being in contact with my body. I saw nothing, felt little and was aware only of being totally out of control physically. There was a time when it seemed I wasn't breathing nor was my heart beating. However, these were impressions left to me after I awoke. God knows. Then all of a sudden I was awake in a place where a distant light glowed dimly. That light turned out to be the light at the nurses' station. I did not know where I was, or why I was there. Sitting up, I found some irritating constraints to my movement. It was when I started to remove tubes and wires from my body that the nurse appeared. She immediately began to assess my condition, asking me questions to see how much I was aware of. How many children do I have? "Why I have three children, one boy and three girls." It took me a little while to come around completely.

From that moment I began to get better. My signs were changing so quickly that they needed to check my blood etc. several times a day just to keep up. The first meal they put in front of me was not very appetizing. It was a bowl of green grams (sort of like lentils) without the benefit of salt, oil, or any type of seasoning. Nevertheless I emptied the bowl. My condition steadily improved. Dr. Warshaw spoke to me soon after I awoke. "We are all glad you're alive, Reverend he smiled, "but we have no idea how you did this. You are a miracle."

Word of my miracle got around quickly and it was normal for someone to stop in just to see me. "Oh, you are the man who had the miraculous healing," they would say, "We heard about you".

I would be remiss if I did not tell of the vision God gave me soon after I came out of the coma. It was a vision describing how I was delivered from the death my doctors knew was inevitable. God showed me a battlefield littered with the rubble of war. I was lying face down in the midst of the carnage, and I was clearly dying. Thrust into my back was a flag pole, with a banner attached. "The flag is not a wound to you," a voice spoke, "It is a symbol of my claim on your life. Because you have obeyed me and done my will, you belong to me." My gaze was then directed to an angel standing near by. He looked like a powerful soldier. "The angel is here because of the flag," the voice spoke again. "He is here to protect my territory." I watched as the angel beckoned, and people began to gather around me in a complete circle. Each one of them was carrying his standard, and as they came close they thrust them into the ground around me until it was bristling with banners. "These are the people who have been praying for you", the familiar voice announced. I was greatly comforted for a moment, and then I was shown the ghastly visage of the devil. He was creeping toward me with a look of absolute confidence as he approached. Coming to finish me, he was not aware of what awaited him just over the next rise. His confidence vanished and his faced revealed only terror as he saw the host that surrounded me with their banners coloring the breeze. He turned and fled in fear as the Lord spoke to me one last time: "The name of the Lord will be feared from the east even unto the west…and when the enemy shall come in like a flood, the spirit of the Lord shall raise a **standard** against him." The devil is no match for the authority of praying men and women!

With daily improvement I was moved to a regular room from the High Dependency Unit. Soon after I moved into the new room, someone was admitted to the room next to mine. The first night we could plainly hear the troubled sounds of fretful crying and loud persuasion for quite a while. Actually I was a bit irritated that they made so much noise. Finally the chaotic chatter stopped and I went to sleep. In the meantime I found out what was going on. Two men came to my room. They were Hindus; one was the husband of the troubled patient and the other was her brother. They explained to me that Kundip, the troubled patient, was dying. She could not see and was not eating. The doctor (Dr. Warshaw again) had done many tests and could not find the source of her problem. They had heard about my miraculous healing and at this point they were ready to receive help from any quarter. The next day, still very weak, I saw the two men standing out in the waiting area across from my room. Going to them, I put my hands on their shoulders and prayed a simple prayer. I knew her problem was a demonic attack and certainly believed that God was able to deliver. "Lord, you are the organizer of all our thoughts. Kundip is in that room, and she can't see or even eat. The doctor doesn't know what to do for her and she is dying. So in Jesus name, fix it." With that

I went down the hall. The next morning the two men burst into my room. "She can see!" they exulted. A while later they were back. "She is eating a meal!" A while later I saw Kundip walking down the hall past my room.

Later I heard Kundip talking, no longer in fretful outbursts but in calm conversation. Walking by herself, talking peacefully, seeing and eating, she was released from the hospital before I was! Before she was released, her brother and husband came once more to my room. Lying in bed, I was a bit appalled as they took my picture. "We know that you are a great holy man because of this miracle you have done", they said. "But we have a question to ask you: What level of the spirit world do you operate in?" I had never been asked a question quite like that. "Well, I operate in the Holy Ghost. Whatever level you need to be, the Holy Ghost is there." They nodded their heads and thanked me again for what God had done. We saw Kundip some time later and she was just fine.

All of these things were certainly a wonder to me, but the greatest of all came one day when I was in the room all alone. I had some long talks with the Lord during this time, but this day was different. All I can say is that it seemed like Jesus walked into the room. As He began to speak with me a holy awe settled over me. "I have allowed all this to happen to you because I want you to be close to me. I want you to be my friend. Will you be my friend?" Tears of joy and wonder ran down my cheeks as I thought of what had been spoken to me. "Is that possible?" I asked. The Lord spoke so kindly, "It is the reason for the Gospel you preach, for

Calvary and all that I do with men. I want you to be my friend." As I tearfully accepted the wonderful offer of my Friend, I began to realize that I would never be the same.

Some time later I was released from the doctors' care. He had told me early on that I would need a year of bed rest to recuperate and that because of severe liver damage I would be on a very limited diet the rest of my life. When I went to his office for the last time, I asked him about my diet. "Oh, you can eat anything you want", he told me. "You have no liver damage whatsoever".

It is impossible to describe that grace that came to us...We learned many lessons that day, but foremost in our minds was the fact that Jesus was more precious than any possession.

Out of the Ashes

How wonderful it was to be on our way home again! We had been in Nairobi for close to ninety days before the doctor finally released me. It took all that time and more for me to regain my strength. Going down the familiar road to Moshi, we wondered at the goodness of God in our lives. "A scripture is on my mind", I told Bonnie. "I keep thinking of it. It says something like, 'You have been called, not only to believe, but to suffer for His sake.' Somehow suffering in the will of God doesn't seem to be unreasonable or fearsome at all." We wondered at this and discussed it further while we hurried down the highway. Finally we arrived in Moshi and stepped into our house for the first time in many weeks.

It was so pleasant to be back at home. We slept in our own bed, drank our own water and just generally enjoyed the ease of being in our own place.

The next morning Bonnie went busily about trying to catch up on a dozen things at once. Predictably the electricity went off, making things a little difficult. I couldn't help much, but I could turn on the generator and restore the power. Alas, the generator was out of gas. No matter, there was a jerry can full in the storage shed. We had a closed in back porch where the generator was kept. It was set up to operate from there, and we had never had any problem of fumes, let alone fire. As I opened the jerry can, I noticed two large pots of dog food that had been cooked. Since we had a strict rule about not cooking on the porch, I guessed that they had just been placed there to cool. Unknown to me both pots were sitting on kerosene cookers, with the fire on (the help figured that rules are to be kept when the boss is watching, and they got into some bad habits). Opening the jerry can I heard the hiss of air under pressure being vented into the room. Drops of gasoline were spewed onto the concrete floor, and fumes began to spread unseen. Soon the fumes caught and a small blaze erupted on the floor in front of me. Realizing the danger, I grabbed a burlap bag and began to smother the flames. Just then our watchman appeared and I instructed him to take hold of another sack and help me put out the fire. What went on in his mind I probably will never know. All I know is that when I looked behind me he had a burlap bag in his hand and the jerry can was tipped over. Immediately flames shot from the floor to the ceiling. I was positioned between the wall and the flames, with the door behind the fire. There was nothing to do but take a deep breath and run through the flames. "Everybody out!" I shouted as I stood by the only door to the house not locked. Bonnie whisked by and I went outside to behold the flames taking hold of the roof. "Is everybody out?"

I asked Bonnie. She replied that they were, and I jumped into the car to go for the fire brigade. Going clear across town I reached the fire station and we were allotted a two man crew with a Land Rover and a hundred gallons of water pumped through a water hose. Arriving back at the house, I discovered Bonnie with blood dripping down her arm. At my question she explained that there had been others in the house that had not made it out. Trapped in the concrete block house with steel windows and security bars, they could not escape. The only open door was blocked with an inferno fueled by the five gallons of petrol and the dry timbers of the porch. Panicked, they found the keys to another door but were too struck with terror to use them. Bonnie finally broke the glass in one door with her fist, took the keys from them and opened the door for their escape.

We stood by the gate and watched as everything we owned was consumed by the fire. The firemen ran out of water and had to go down the road, contact the water department and get them to open a pipe. Topped off with another hundred gallons of water, they came back for another try. Bonnie prayed for rain as the flames licked the roof into oblivion. Later people around the town commented how they saw a cloud appear and rain descend in just one neighborhood. It was a strange sight indeed. However it was apparently the will of God for us to see the utter destruction of all we possessed, and receive instead the manifold grace of God for our portion. As we stood watching, we individually talked to God about what we beheld. "The Lord gives and the Lord takes away, blessed be the name of the Lord,"

I quoted. "I just want you to know it's all right," I told Him, "I love you". Immediately an unspeakable peace flooded my heart and mind. Bonnie told me later of much the same experience. It is impossible to describe the grace that came to us that day. All we can say is that we wouldn't trade it for a hundred houses. We learned many lessons that day, but foremost in our minds was the fact that Jesus was more precious than any possession.

The fire blazed with such incredible heat that the glass in the windows melted and ran down the concrete block wall. Collections and keepsakes were consumed with the heat of a blaze that seemed intended to take our very lives. The next day the rubble was cool enough to sift through, though little was left unburned. Someone brought my ring of keys to me. Blackened and crusted with soot, they are still in my possession. A few china cups survived the flames, and Bonnie took them for remembrance.

The next Sunday I preached in the Headquarters Church in Moshi. I spoke from Revelation 1:18, blackened keys in hand.

Rev 1:18
18 *I am he that liveth, and was dead; and, behold, I am alive for evermore, Amen; and have the keys of hell and of death.(KJV)*

It seemed the devil had failed to destroy me in Nairobi, and now he had tried to consume me in the fire. But Jesus has the keys of both hell and of death!

Later at our National Conference Bonnie invited the wives of the National Board members for a time of fellowship. There she shared with those ladies the wonderful lesson she had learned from the fiery trial. Giving each of them one of the remaining china cups; she told them that the china did not have to fear the fire because it had already been there. "When you are going through the fire, take down this cup and remember what you are made of," she told them. "You don't have to fear the fire".

*The presence of God flooded the room and we con-
cluded the session with great expectations. Now
the only thing remaining was, how is God going to
answer?*

Effectual Fervent Prayer

An important part of our work as missionaries
was teaching. We held seminars from time to time in
the different areas of the country. This was vital to
developing the spiritual level of the people and leaders
in the nation. One such session took us to Iringa, in the
southern area of Tanzania.

Getting to Iringa was a challenge in itself. We
lived in the northern part of the country, just south of
Mt. Kilimanjaro. From there we traveled the long road
eastward toward Dar es Salaam, and then turned south
into the highlands beyond Morogoro. The road twisted
through sisal plantations and past numerous villages.
It was at that time pocked with many pot holes. The
edges sometimes looked as if a giant tarmac monster
had passed by, taking bites at random from the edge
of the highway. It was a beautiful ride, but tedious as
well.

Brother & Sister Royer had come from Uganda to
visit and take part in the seminar. Bro. Royer and I
made the 800 kilometer trek (500 miles) and finally

landed in Iringa exhausted but glad to be off the road. We checked in to the Ismailia Hotel, certainly not a grand place but the best we could find.

The seminar was being held in a borrowed facility in Iringa town. Pastors and church leaders from the region had come in for the meeting. They were staying in a rented house, cooking their own meals and eating together. The inhabitants of this area are a likable people. They came joyfully and co-operated the best they could in whatever needed to be done. This area was far from many of our other churches in Tanzania and they didn't get as much attention as we would have liked to have given them.

Everyone gathered in as the seminar began and Brother Royer and I took turns teaching. We would go for about three hours in a session, dividing the time between us. These people were hungry for the word and soaked in everything we taught.

Desiring to make an impact spiritually as well as grounding them in the doctrine, I planned to teach on praying in the spirit. The time for that session arrived, and as I looked into their earnest faces I silently prayed for an anointing to deliver this important message.

Years before we had spent time in Wheeling, West Virginia, under the mentoring of Brother Billy Cole. There we learned vital lessons in faith, ministering in the spirit, spiritual warfare and the like. It was an invaluable boost to our lives and ministry. Now was the time to share a bit of this blessing with the people of Iringa.

Taking my text, I spoke of the power of the spirit in our prayers. Sometimes we don't even know what to pray, but the spirit does. From time to time we must travail in prayer in order to bring things to birth. Many think of this as a very special ministry for only the most spiritual. In that mindset they count themselves out, thinking that such a thing is too high for them. However, the scripture tells us that God has given the manifestation of the spirit to every man to profit withal. Powerful praying in the spirit is certainly available to anyone who has received the Holy Ghost.

As I neared the end of the lesson, I challenged my pupils to put this knowledge to work. We would select a prayer request and all of us would focus on that one thing. Then, with an earnest desire for that specific answer, we would begin to pray in our own language. Keeping the request firmly in our thinking, we would then begin to pray in the spirit, speaking with other tongues. As we began to pray in the spirit, many of us would enter into travail, being bowed down in spiritual labor for the answer to be delivered to us. After some consultation they gave their unified request; that God would bring souls to our meeting, and that they would be saved. This was a wonderful aspiration, and certainly one founded in faith. We had not advertised the meeting to outsiders, and this was the next to last session in the seminar. No doubt about it, if this happened we would know that God did it.

Going to prayer exactly as they were taught, these sweet people were soon in the throes of praying in the spirit. Most of them entered into travailing prayer. It was a powerful time of intercession. Just to watch their earnest petitioning was a joyful thing for this teacher. The presence of God flooded the room and we concluded the session with great expectations. Now the only thing remaining was, how is God going to answer;

We broke for lunch and went our ways. We had one more session in the afternoon. Brother Royer taught the first session, and it was received with joy; then came the last session of the seminar. As I called the class to order, four ladies entered the room. No one here knew them, but in African fashion folks just moved over and made room for the new pupils. These ladies were from the Masai tribe and were decked out in purple garments, with beaded necklaces and long earrings dangling from pierced ears.

As I taught the class it was obvious to all that God had answered our prayers. Without invitation, announcement or explanation these ladies had been led of the spirit into our meeting. Coming to the end of the final session, it seemed that God was not done. "We have been blessed today with visitors to our session", I spoke. "We should bless these ladies in return." Beckoning them to come and stand in the front, I thanked the ladies for coming and told them that I would like to pray a blessing upon them. They were glad for this and came willingly. After a few minutes two of those women were speaking with other tongues!

Brother Royer taught, Brother Ward exhorted and God gave the object lesson. Effectual fervent prayer availeth much!

I made the call and got directions to the house where Pop was staying. Setting a time, I went with a prayer for salvation for this man I had never met.

Pop Jordan's Salvation

Pastor Harold Hoffman had been giving Pop Jordan a Bible Study. This was something Bro. Hoffman did so well. You could just about count on it every time; if Brother Hoffman gave a Bible Study, somebody was getting baptized. This time is was Pop Jordan, a man in his seventies who was dying of cancer.

Brother Hoffman called me one day and asked if I would go to pray with Pop Jordan. "If you pray with him I know he will get the Holy Ghost", he urged. "Sure, I will be glad to go", I replied. This was something I was always glad to do.

I made the call and got directions to the house where Pop was staying. Setting a time, I went with a prayer for salvation for this man I had never met.

Arriving at the house I was ushered upstairs to a pleasant room equipped with oxygen and other medical equipment. This was where Pop would live out his days, though he was making plans to go fishing, never capitulating to the rigors of disease. He was an easy person to meet, and soon we were engaged in conversation. I knew he was from Tennessee, and my family was from Kentucky, so we spoke of things we had in common. From sorghum molasses and biscuits to country churches and old hymns the conversation flowed easily.

After easily getting acquainted with Pop, I turned to the purpose of my visit. "Pop, I have come here today to pray with you to receive the Holy Ghost" I began, "Would you like that?" "Oh yes," he replied. He was ready to receive. I then explained to him just what we were going to do. "God lives in our praises, Pop. When we praise the Lord, He just comes near." Explaining to him just what that worship was comprised of; I told him that he would speak with tongues when the Holy Ghost came to him. He was fine with that, though he had never seen it before. Just before we began to worship, I told Pop that first the Holy Ghost would fill the room, as it did on the Day of Pentecost. We would feel the spirit when that happened, and that meant it was time to receive.

We began by singing some old familiar hymns which Pop knew very well. Quickly the sweet presence of Jesus filled the room where the old man lay. "Alright Pop, do you feel the spirit of God in this room?" "Oh yes," he replied, "I feel it." I helped him to raise his hands and gave him a few words of instruction as to how he should worship the Lord. Placing my hand upon his brow, we joined our voices in praise to the Lord. Before long Pop was worshipping earnestly, obviously moved by the spirit of God. Soon the bed began to shake as the weak old gentleman shook under the power of the Holy Ghost. Words of another tongue sprang from his lips as Pop got his baptism in the spirit.

That night Brother Hoffman baptized Pop Jordan in the biggest bath tub I ever saw. Weak in body, Pop was joyful in his spirit. It was a happy conclusion to his day of salvation.

In subsequent visits Pop shared with me his desire to lead his children to this same salvation. Within a few short months Pop was gone. As it happened I was needed to preach his funeral. His son Tommy was chosen to represent the family with a few words about Pop. Tommy told how he used to help his Dad work on the car. His chief duty was to hold the light for him. How fitting that Tommy walks with God today, carrying on the light that Pop Jordan possessed in his last days.

"Tomorrow I have a lunch appointment with Bro. Roach", I told them. "I will give him this prayer cloth and I believe God will heal him."

Saving the Sick

Jim Roach pastored across town. He didn't belong to the same church we did, but he knew and preached the message. Once we had some special services and Bro. Roach came to the meeting. He was new to the town and new to us, and it was good to meet him.

From time to time he would visit with us, and we became friends. In the course of getting to know one another we learned that Jim Roach, about forty years old, was in the fourth stage of Hodgkin's disease. This troubled us as we felt compassion for a man of his years facing almost certain death. It just seemed like there ought to be something we could do about it; and there was. We could pray.

As an associate Pastor in Sterling Heights, Michigan, it fell to my lot to give the Bible study one Wednesday evening. Feeling directed to teach on intercessory prayer, I made a plan to appeal to God for Jim Roach.

The lesson was received with faith by the good saints in Sterling Heights. They were almost all aware of Brother Roach's condition, and they were concerned.

The word spoke of effectual prayer, prayer in the spirit, travailing prayer. Simple instructions made the way plain for all to approach the throne to receive God's grace.

As the lesson ended we brought a prayer cloth to be anointed. Gathering the saints around, I gave them simple instructions in how to pray this prayer. The saints responded with earnest petitions. Many of them prayed fervently in the spirit, laboring in the travail of birth for Jim's answer. At the close of the prayer I took the prayer cloth in my hand, showing it to all the church. "Tomorrow I have a lunch appointment with Brother Roach", I told them. "I will give him this prayer cloth and I believe God will heal him".

We met at the Ram's Horn restaurant the next day. It was crowded with customers as we settled down into a booth for our meal. We talked of different things and generally had a pleasant visit, but this was not why I was there. Finally, toward the end of our lunch, I gave him the prayer cloth. I don't know what I expected him to do, but frankly I was disappointed at the casual way he stuffed it into his pocket. "Thanks, here let me pick up the tab. Maybe we can get together again sometime", he spoke. I wondered if that was it. Is this all we get for tearful travail for his healing? Oh well, I thought, we did our part. Now it is up to him and God.

Waiting for a couple of days, I tried to call Brother Roach, but there was no answer. I wanted to give a victory report on Sunday, but it was not to be. I couldn't find Jim Roach.

Finally on Monday I called his church office to learn that he was called out of town because of his fathers' illness. "Well, how is Brother Roach doing," I asked. "Oh, haven't you heard?" the church secretary replied, "He was in the church on Sunday, running the aisles shouting, I'm healed, I'm healed!" He had told the church that when he reached his house after our lunch together, he put the prayer cloth on his body. Immediately he felt as if a cloud lifted off of him, and he was completely healed!

After a bit we heard voices joining with the beating of a drum. Through the open windows we could see a group of people dancing around the church, with the witch doctor in the lead.

If the Devil Doesn't Like it...

Three hours from our home in Kakamega, Kenya, we arrived in the area of sugar plantations in the southwest. We met Brother Arthur Bukatchi, the presbyter of the region, who had arranged for the service to be held that day in a village quite near the Tanzania border. This was our occupation much of the time, traveling to villages and towns for Holy Ghost rallies.

This particular day was sunny and warm as we left the tarmac and bounced along the dirt roads in our Isuzu Trooper. The air conditioning didn't work, and the roads were dusty. We often arrived back home with hair tinted to match the red soil. This was a minor inconvenience compared to some of the rigors of travel in Africa. Staying in places like Gilleys Hotel (a no-star establishment in Migori) or the Ismailia in Iringa was pure adventure. Getting out of bed in the dark just wasn't done in some of these places because part of the time the African wildlife didn't stay outdoors.

Arriving at the intended village, we climbed out of the Trooper, stretched ourselves to take out some of the kinks brought on by the bumpy roads, and took a look around. It was pretty much your run of the mill African village; children chasing a worn out tire with a stick in their hand to keep it rolling, chickens pretty much having the run of the place and the smoke of cooking fires blowing in the gentle breeze. It was a place the devil claimed, and we were not there with his permission.

The church was built in the manner of so many village churches. The walls were of mud, with perhaps a window or two on each side of the building. You don't put a lot of windows in a mud building. It weakens the structure. This one sported a tin roof, which put it a cut above some of the grass-roofed varieties. It also made for a warmer building as the people packed in and the sun glared down on it. The floor was the usual mud surface, swept clean of dust and other offending detritus. With guests coming, it had been spruced up as much as they were able to manage, with a few fresh-picked flowers adorning the platform and a freshly washed and ironed cloth covering the pulpit.

When we reached the church and were about to enter, a messenger approached Brother Bukatchi. I stood by patiently as they spoke in soft tones. The messenger looked from me to the church building and back to Bro. Bukatchi. I knew something was up but also knew I would find out when they had time to work out what to do.

"The Pastor has sent a message that he can't come to the service today," he relayed to me. Thinking that perhaps he was ill or had some problem, I waited to hear the story. To my surprise the presbyter went on, "The witch doctor has warned him not to go to the church today, and he is afraid". I looked around and saw people filing into the church. Evidently the word had not gotten out about this challenge, or the warning was only for him. I looked to Brother Bukatchi to see what his reaction would be. "I think we should go ahead and have church," he said. It was clear he was not pleased with the pastor. "How can you claim to be a pastor and be afraid of the witch doctor"? How indeed!

As we entered the service, singing was already in progress. Brother Bukatchi stepped into the pastors' role for the day and the proceedings went as usual. Eventually I was ushered to the pulpit and introduced as the Missionary and preacher for the day. The crowd was not very big, but I had never been here before and could not tell if it was a normal group for them or down because of the witch doctor's threatening.

Taking my text I waded into my message with Brother Bukatchi faithfully interpreting. About half way through my sermon I heard some commotion outside and raised my voice a bit in order to be heard. The noise was clearly moving in our direction. After a bit we heard voices joining with the beating of a drum. Through the open windows we could see a group of people dancing around the church, with the witch doctor in the lead. This went on for a while and as I preached there was certainly a battle in the heavenlies; angel and demon vying for the pre-eminence.

Eventually the drummer and dancers left, leaving the church and the victory to us. At the end of the altar prayer we counted nine who had received the Holy Ghost out of a crowd of 25 to 30 in the church. Brother Bukatchi was ecstatic. "Brother Ward, this is a miracle!" he enthused. "We have never had anyone receive the Holy Ghost in this church before. All we ever do is fight devils!" I turned to him and spoke, "That is your problem, Brother. God called us to preach, not fuss with devils. Just do what God called you to do and let God deal with the devil." Apparently he had a few ideas about how he was going to deal with the Pastor, but I prudently left that to him.

So we learned the lesson; do what God called you to do, and if the devil doesn't like it...

...I looked at my watch; time to go. No choir, no testimonies, no preaching; just a short greeting and maybe a couple of announcements was the order of the day.

A Short Stop in Serari

We didn't often get visitors in Tanzania. Maybe someone would come for our Conference, a visiting speaker or two. Tanzania was sort of out of the way; you had to go there on purpose or you wouldn't ever land there.

One year we determined to remedy this situation and invited about twenty guests to join us for Conferences, Crusades, Seminars and the like. Normally out of this many invitations a handful would actually make the trip. That year almost every one we invited accepted the invitation and actually came! We were stunned. Six months of company enriched the lives of the Ward family in that twelve months, and we were blessed with ministry of every form and fashion.

One such visitor was a pastor from Tennessee. He was a diminutive fireball of a preacher with a passion for God. He spoke with the soft southern drawl of central Tennessee, and spoke the colorful language of a log truck driver, which is what he was.

We had a great time teaching a seminar in Moshi, at the headquarters church. Then we embarked on a trip through Kenya to reach the western extreme of Tanzania, on the shores of Lake Victoria. Going through Kenya definitely made for a longer journey, but the state of the roads through the Serengeti made it doubtful whether we would reach our destination in good order.

Our final destination was a church located between Musoma and Mwanza, two major cities on the lake. Preparing the itinerary, I remembered that we would pass right by our church in Serari, just over the border from Kenya. We had not been to that church or even the area for a long time. "We will be passing your church on the way to dedicate Brother Okiro's new building," I told them. "We cannot stay for a service but we would be pleased to stop for a while and greet you". With that we departed for the long trip to Serari and beyond.

We crossed the Kenya-Tanzania border just beyond Suna Migori. Our church in Serari was just on the other side of the border post. Moving slowly out of the no man's land, we crossed the border, I peered to my right, looking for the turn to the church. I was fearful of missing the turn and knew it was close. As we approached the dirt track leading off of the highway it was obvious where we should turn. Waiting by the path was a congregation of people. They had come out to the road to greet us and to escort us to our destination. Running along side the car, trilling their greetings to us, they greatly enhanced my feelings of guilt for planning such a brief visit.

Arriving at the church, we disembarked and followed the entourage into the stone church. The pastor was waiting for us, all smiles. I repeated to him that it was not possible for us to stay very long, because Brother Okiro was waiting about two hours away for us to dedicate his church building. No choir, no testimonies, no preaching; just a short greeting and maybe a couple of announcements was the order of the day.

True to the plan, the pastor introduced us quickly. I stood to greet the people, shared some announcements with them of future events and introduced my guest. "Just give us a few words, brother", I said, bringing him to the pulpit. He cooperated and I looked at my watch; time to go. Standing again in front of the people I opened my mouth to tell them farewell and pray a dismissal prayer. "Don't leave," urged the spirit. "These people need the Holy Ghost." Sensing a higher authority than my itinerary could boast, I submitted to the leading of the spirit of God.

"Is there anybody here who would like to receive the Holy Ghost today?" I asked. About a third of the congregation raised their hands. Bringing them to the front, we arranged an altar prayer. No singing, no preaching, no testimonies or prayer, just an altar service. After giving the seekers a few instructions we began to worship, with the ministers going about to lay hands on the seekers. We prayed with them for about ten to fifteen minutes. When we counted those who were speaking with other tongues, we were amazed to see that fifteen of them had been spirit filled!

Having obeyed the leading of the spirit and reaping the harvest there, we continued with our plan. After a short dismissal prayer we resolutely marched back to our car before they could invite us to lunch. Waving at the happy congregation, we found our way back to the road. My guest just shook his head for a good while, marveling at what God had done.

About two hours and many pot holes later we arrived at the church of Brother Okiro. Our visitor preached the message of dedication. Several choirs sang and many testimonies filled up the service schedule. About two hours later we felt again the moving of the spirit, and twelve more Tanzanians were filled with the Holy Ghost. Many such stories were acted out that year as God gave us what we asked for over and over.

Twenty guests, six months of visitors, surely a record for our harvest field, but none of them topped the joy of the momentary detour, the short stop in Serari.

*I wondered what miracle of transformation would
make me the powerful evangelist who could fulfill
such a task. "No", the voice came back, "you do not
have to be great; I am great.":.*

My "Not So Great" Job Description

January, 1987 found us at the Annual Conference of
the UPC of Kenya. This meeting was held in Nairobi
as usual and we were busy with board meetings,
services, prayer meetings, etc. We always finished the
Conference "running on fumes" but blessed.

This particular morning we managed to get to the
early prayer meeting on time. It was the beginning of
the year and we wondered what the next twelve months
would hold for us. Never very good at waiting, I urged
the Lord to fill me in on what the next year held for
us. "What do you want me to do this year?" I prayed.
"Just give me a job description and I will know what
to do".

Now some folks speak of knowing for years ahead
where God is going to take them, what they will be
doing, etc. That is definitely not how God had dealt
with us over the years. I guess the Lord knows we
would run out and try to get done whatever He showed

us to do. Most often we got our instructions when it was time to do it. Our penchant for planning, arranging, preparing, etc. was not considered, so we just got over it.

Hearing from God is always a thrill. He doesn't have to pay attention to us. He isn't required to respond to our impatient urging. But this day He did. "What I want you to do this year is that, in the services you preach, you should have one thousand people receive the Holy Ghost", my answer came immediately. Wow; I was impressed! Thinking of the ramifications of such a task, it was instantly apparent to me that I couldn't do it. But here was God telling me what to do. Me and my big mouth!

"Well, Lord, if that is what you want me to do, then it is clear that something has to change. I have never had one thousand people receive the Holy Ghost in one year before", I countered. "I guess I will have to grow and change. I will have to become something great!" I wondered what miracle of transformation would make me the powerful evangelist who could fulfill such a task. "No", the voice came back, "you do not have to be great; I am great." Now there was a revelation; working as a team, only one of us had to be big and powerful and all knowing. God was already all of those things and more. Without new methods, lacking any new equipment or technology I could get the job done as long as I showed up with my great co-worker: interesting.

Well for twelve months we watched God work. In that entire year we never had a crowd bigger than two hundred people, and the average was probably closer to seventy or seventy-five per service. We had services in mud churches, under trees, in the market; just wherever we landed.

That year was a difficult one in many ways. It was an election year, so on several occasions our service was cancelled in order to accommodate a political rally. Sometimes sickness made our travels impossible, the car broke down often. The month of July was spent in the US attending my fathers' funeral and spending some time with the family. We averaged preaching once a week that year with all of these problems. Not so great for an evangelist.

It would be nice to speak of great gatherings, eloquent preaching, etc., but the fact is we just kept putting one foot in front of the other. Some days when the message was finished, I would realize what a mediocre job I had made of preaching. Some times it would have been much preferable to just dismiss and go home. However in that year God taught us a vital lesson. He does not change; not ever. Regardless of how much I felt that I had dropped the ball, no matter how quiet it was when I finished; God was not in any way weakened or deterred from accomplishing His purpose. "Well, Lord, that is what I can do", I would pray, "Now let's see what you can do." Continuing as if everything was just wonderful, over and over again God showed up and people received the Holy Ghost. I didn't have to be great. His strength is made perfect in weakness.

Knowing that no sickness can diminish His ability to heal, no sin can take away the power of His cleansing blood is a wonderful comfort. Between us, we and

Jesus know everything and we have all power. It is OK to be weak, as long as we are connected with God.

Oh yes, that year we saw God fill 1,019 people with the Holy Ghost!

Eph 6:10
10 *Finally, my brethren, be strong in the Lord, and in the power of his might.(KJV)*

Suddenly I became aware that the car was not re-sponding to the steering wheel. Going about 60 miles an hour downhill in a heavily populated area was frightening to say the least.

Going with God Behind the Wheel

Our 1986 Isuzu Trooper was made in Kenya. Soon after we got the car it became obvious that we had a lemon. We would find nuts lying under the front seat where they had fallen off the bolts which secured the seats to the chassis. The odd part would occasionally come loose, as it seemed they must have had a shortage of lock washers the day this car was assembled. The air conditioning unit we purchased and installed worked fine as long as we could keep it attached to the vehicle. Our jury-rigged bracket just couldn't stand the strain and so we gave up on it and rolled down the windows.

One day we had quite a struggle getting home from church as the car bucked and kicked, traveling along in fits and starts. Finally reaching home, I lifted the hood and took a look at the carburetor. In my slight understanding of mechanics I thought that something didn't look right. Removing the breather I took hold of the carburetor and it came off in my hand. We must have kept several angels hopping just keeping us on the road.

Missionary business on a sunny day took me to Kitale, in the Kenya highlands. After making contact with the presbyter of the area, I started on my way home. I was glad to be able to get back on the same day without having to travel in the dark. Now somehow over the years as a Missionary I had gotten the reputation of being a fast driver. I offer no defense, while admitting to nothing. Hurrying out of Kitale, I headed down a hill which took me past a busy market place. Suddenly I became aware that the car was not responding to the steering wheel. Going about 60 miles an hour downhill in a heavily populated area was frightening to say the least. My greatest fear was that someone would appear in my path and I would not be able to do anything about it. Breathing a prayer I did my best to get the vehicle to the side of the road safely. To step on the brakes or try to turn the wheel drastically would possibly throw me into a turn I could do nothing about. Amazingly the car slowed gently, pulling slightly to the side, so that I ended up parked safely without hitting anything or anyone. Thank God!

After a long wait a tow truck appeared and pulled my car to a garage. It turned out that the connecting rod between the front wheels had snapped in two, leaving me with virtually no control of the vehicle. It was a total miracle that I had come to a safe stop without turning one of the wheels contrary to the other and losing control completely. God is good.

Well, it would take about a week to get a new connecting rod, so I ended up staying at the Bongo Hotel in Kitale. The rod could be welded and re-installed the following day. With those repairs I limped home the next day, careful to avoid putting undue stress on the car.

A couple of days later I found a replacement rod in Kisumu and had it installed. As was my custom, I did not throw away the old rod. You never throw away any working parts in Africa. You kept them for spares when you broke down the next time in some remote place.

Some time later we were on our way to a rally near the Uganda border. With me in the car were several preachers from the area. Going down a nice stretch of highway, we overtook a car ahead of us. Passing the vehicle we were sailing along at about 65 miles per hour or so when I turned the wheel to pull back into our own lane. Instead of making the easy drift back into the lane, the car did a sideways maneuver that I had never seen a car do before. Slowing gradually, we pulled into a side road for a look. My brand new connecting rod had broken again. Pulling the welded rod out of the trunk, I sent the preachers on to the rally while I got the old rod re-installed.

Eventually I found a mechanic who discovered why this was happening. His explanation was a bit over my head as he talked of parts I had never heard of.

Twice, going down the road at speed, I had escaped certain danger if not death. Twice the car behaved as if someone else was guiding it safely off the road. When God takes something out of your hands, let Him do it. He is a better driver than you are.

"You see, someone died nearby a couple of days ago and today is the funeral", they offered, Everybody has gone to the funeral. They left us behind to take care of you."

A Divine Switch

Off to another service, I bid goodbye to Bonnie, "Look for me when you see me". You just never knew what might happen and how long it would take when you went to church out of town. This trip was taking me to Webuye, a little over an hour from home. The road was good, the day was pretty and it just looked like it would be a good day. Little did I know what the day held for me.

Arriving at the planned site of the meeting, I was somewhat disappointed to find only some children and a couple of ladies from the church present. Oh well, just be patient and some folks will come; they always do. After waiting an hour or so I was called to lunch. The ladies served up a nice meal of ugali and kuku, the local "Sunday" dinner. After a polite interval they informed me that no one was coming for the service. "You see, someone died nearby a couple of days ago and today is the funeral", they offered, "Everybody has gone to the funeral. They left us behind to take care of you".

Well, my first thought was go home; cut your losses, you have lots to do. Then the gentle voice of the spirit suggested that I go to the funeral. "Would it be alright if I went to the funeral?" I asked. The ladies responded that they would go along with me to show the way. So it was that I arrived a short time later at the funeral of someone I had never met. I wasn't even sure how to act. Finding the family of the deceased, I offered my condolences and took a place in the shade with some other men. My plan was to just sit and wait to see what God would do. I had fulfilled my part by just showing up.

Before too long I was approached by a gentleman who asked me if I was a Missionary. When I confessed to that, he requested me to preach to the gathering. No problem, I could do that. So they gathered the people together. They came willingly. They had been sitting around here for a couple of days by now and this was a welcome diversion for many of them.

I don't remember what I preached, but that was not the most important thing to me. This was an opportunity to make an altar call and pray for some people. That was why I had come.

Well, after it was all done we counted fourteen people who were speaking with other tongues for the first time in their lives.

Leaving the funeral, we returned to the originally planned site for the meeting. The ladies returned with me along with several others from the church. Of course it was unthinkable to leave without having some "chai". This is tea made with about half milk and a load of sugar. The Kenyans love it and never pass up a chance to stop for chai.

Finally taking my leave of them, I got in my car and turned the ignition key; nothing. Nothing that is, except a pathetic groan from the starter followed by a deathly silence. It began to look like I would spend the night in this place.

Then I recalled having had a similar problem when I was a home missionary in Connecticut. For a period of about six weeks, my car would run just fine all week until Sunday morning. Then, hurrying on our way to church, we would get the same hopeless noise I was now hearing. Finally I would speak in my sternest voice, "Devil, get your hands off my car. Car, start in Jesus name". It worked every time, until the devil decided to let it go and try something else.

This was just what I decided to do now. Rebuking the devil for causing this nuisance, I commanded the car to start in Jesus name. It started immediately.

God had switched the venue of our meeting, filling fourteen strangers with the Holy Ghost at a funeral. Then He resurrected my car so that I could return home. Going down the road toward Kakamega, I allowed that it had turned out to be a pretty good day after all.

Finishing the prayer, it seemed not much had taken place, but I felt to speak a word of faith to her. "From this moment you will begin to get better", I spoke. I still had no idea what her problem was.

Restored

Brother Harold Strange is a unique man of God. Delivered from a life bound for hell, he was mentored by a godly man, Pastor Clifford Murray. Brother Murray taught Harold to live like a Christian. Before long he was called to preach. He successfully preached as an Evangelist for a number of years, and found himself following his beloved mentor as Pastor of Apostolic Lighthouse Tabernacle in Massillon, Ohio.

I have had the privilege of preaching in that church on a number of occasions. Among the many things you expect when you go there is undivided attention to the word, earnest prayer in the altar, and miracles of healing. Armed with faith and a clear understanding of the word, Brother Strange often ministers in miracles of healing.

One exception was an older lady in his church who complained of not being able to sleep. "You mean you never get any sleep?" the Pastor queried. "Not really, she replied, only sometimes in church." One way or another you were going to get what you needed at Lighthouse Tabernacle.

Preaching in Massillon is something I love to do. Results in the altar is what we usually see when we get to be there. This night was special though, for God worked a mighty miracle.

Now this church has not succumbed to the peer pressures of churches around them. While most of the churches start at 6 PM or so on Sunday evening, Lighthouse Tabernacle starts at 7:45 PM. They like it that way, and it works. Singing from the hymnal is alive and well in Massillon. They find it sufficient to have one song leader standing behind the pulpit, no praise team, thank you. What they do have is spirit filled worship, anointed preaching and faith for miracles. Who cares if they don't get home on Sunday night until midnight?

On this particular occasion I was not the preacher for the service. I had brought another preacher to them and he was the preacher for that night.

Following the preaching the saints lined the altar from wall to wall as usual. We moved among them, praying for various needs. As I progressed to the second and third line of people in the front of the church, I noticed a lady sitting about two rows back. Not knowing what her need was, I felt impressed to pray for her. Finishing the prayer, it seemed not much had taken place, but I felt to speak a word of faith to her. "From this moment you will begin to get better", I spoke. I still had no idea what her problem was.

A few days later I called Pastor Strange from another city. "Do you remember that lady you prayed for Sunday night?" he asked. Then he began to tell me her story. She had suffered long from fibromyalgia, a disease that brought excruciating pain and bone degeneration. For some time she had used pain medication constantly. Her limbs had been affected to the point that she could only stand and walk with the use of heavy braces. Long illness had affected her spirit, and she was known by her illness. "She came to church Wednesday night, walking without braces, having no pain and changed in mind and spirit", he reported. God had worked a marvelous healing without fanfare or excitement, keeping all the glory to Himself, as it should be.

A month later I saw Brother Strange at the Camp Meeting. "Remember that lady you prayed for?" he asked. "She was at the park running around like nothing had ever troubled her. Her kneecaps had degenerated to the size of marbles, and now they are whole!"

Looking down at Nathanael, she saw him close one eye, then the other, smile and move his baby face in perfect order. The second opinion had arrived.

A Second Opinion

Nathanael was born to Jared and Lindsey Banta early in 2004. He was a beautiful child and much appreciated in the home of Jared and Lindsey. Grandma and Grandpa Banta weren't offended at all by this most recent addition to their clan. Everything went fine for them until one night he became dreadfully ill.

No matter what they did, his fever would not stay down. After doing everything they knew how to do they took their baby to the hospital, where he was treated and finally released. With several days of treatment Nathanael seemed to be out of the woods and he was released from the hospital on Tuesday. Ten or twelve minutes after returning home, Nathanael started having seizures. Racing back to the hospital, Jared and Lindsey were more than concerned. Their darling first born was dangerously ill. He had two more seizures that night.

A CAT scan showed serious problems from the disease. The diagnosis was chilling. Bacterial meningitis was attacking Nathanaels' brain. Explaining the results of the CAT scan, the doctor told them, "Your baby has serious damage to his brain. On a scale of one to ten, with ten being perfect, your child may be a two or three." At this point Nathanaels' parents and all who loved him went to the throne of God for a second opinion.

Nathanaels' head came under increased pressure as the brain lining failed to process the fluid in his cranium. This was drained on Thursday and an appointment was made to insert a permanent drain the following Tuesday. They expected to need to drain the fluid every day until then. By Friday there was no need to drain the fluid and the surgery to insert the drain was cancelled.

On Saturday Nathanael was scheduled for another MRI. We visited the hospital that day. When we arrived we found the Mother and Father and both Grandmothers in the room. While we were there Pastor Clark Baker and his wife Bonnie stopped in along with Brother Randy Langford, the Bantas' pastor. We visited for about an hour.

As we prepared to leave, we gathered around the baby to pray. Approaching the child, I sensed the prompting of the spirit. "No need to pray, just surround the child with praise", the gentle voice said. I expressed this to the others in the room and in one mind we began to worship softly, filling the hospital room with praise. A profound presence of God came and inhabited that praise. We continued for some time, taking comfort and faith from the visitation of the spirit.

Concluding our worship, we all focused on the little child in his Mothers' arms. Then softly Lindsay began to sing, "To God be the glory, to God be the

glory, to God be the glory for the things he has done..."
Eyes wet with tears looked on as this precious Mother
entrusted her firstborn baby to a mighty God. As far as
I am concerned, if Nathanael wasn't healed before that
moment, he was healed right then. The high praises of
God are never ignored.

We took our leave, voicing every encouragement
we could. The next day, the reading of the MRI was
explained to Jared and Lindsey. "Well, your baby
doesn't seem to be as sick as we thought. However,
you have to understand that there has been damage to
the frontal lobe of the brain. This will be evidenced
by a lack of control of his facial expression. Do you
understand?" Lindsey nodded and the doctor left her
to her thoughts. Looking down at Nathanael, she saw
him close one eye, then the other, smile and move his
baby face in perfect order. The second opinion had
arrived.

Nathanael was released the next day. He continued
to show improvement and the parents claimed victory.
Eventually, at about four months old, Nathanael went
for further evaluation. The pictures, hundreds of
them, showed a perfect child. He was being weaned
off the medication and was behaving normally. His
development was moving ahead normally. "Just what
was your baby's problem?" asked the new technician.
Jared answered that Nathanael had contracted bacterial
meningitis. "Are you sure, really sure that is what he
had?" the technician persisted. He went on to explain
that infants almost never survived bacterial meningitis,
and even if they did, they would be physically damaged

by the disease. He had never seen such a complete recovery from this devastating sickness.

They examined the hundreds of MRI images for quite a while, trying to explain what had happened. In the meantime, Nathanael just keeps on growing and acting like a little guy should who just had a miracle.

PS

Somewhere in the process it was noted that the attack on Nathanaels' body had caused shrinking of the brain. There was a clearly discernible space between the skull and the brain, not a normal situation at all. The doctor was quick to explain that, once brain matter is lost, it never regenerates; never. However, the final MRI showed a full cranium, not only healed but fully restored!

Once again we were shown that while faith and obedience bring healing, worship brings restoration.

Books by David B. Ward

Doctrine
> The Common Salvation
> Baptism: The How and the Why
> The Covenant of Holiness

Ministry
> Altar Ministry
> The Means to Revival
> How Does Your Garden Grow?
> The Lord's Prayer for His Church
> Six Fold Ministry
> Thoughts on Growing

Spiritual Development
> Transformed
> Effectual Fervent Prayer
> Judgment With Mercy

Testimony
> Look What the Lord Has Done

Order these books from:
www.MinistryPathways.org

Also on the web site:
Apostolic College of Ministries

Printed in the United States
27631LVS00001B/13-120

9 781420 834222